The Wild World of Animals

Cheetahs

Spotted Speedsters

by Jody Sullivan

Consultant:
Tammy Quist
President
The Wildcat Society

Bridgestone Books
an imprint of Capstone Press
Mankato, Minnesota

Bridgestone Books are published by Capstone Press
151 Good Counsel Drive, P.O. Box 669, Mankato, Minnesota 56002
http://www.capstone-press.com

Library of Congress Cataloging-in-Publication Data
Sullivan, Jody.
    Cheetahs : spotted speedsters / by Jody Sullivan.
    p. cm.—(The wild world of animals)
    Includes bibliographical references (p. 24) and index.
    Summary: A brief introduction to cheetahs, describing their physical characteristics,
habitat, young, food, predators, and relationship to people.
    ISBN 0-7368-1393-4 (hardcover)
    1. Cheetah—Juvenile literature. [1. Cheetah. 2. Endangered species.] I. Title.
II. Series.
QL737.C23 S85 2003
599.75'9—dc21   2001008149

Editorial Credits
Megan Schoeneberger, editor; Karen Risch, product planning editor; Linda Clavel,
    designer; Kelly Garvin, photo researcher

Photo Credits
Ann & Rob Simpson, cover
Corbis/Tom Brakefield, 18
Digital Stock, 1, 4, (texture) cover, 2, 3, 6, 10, 12, 14, 16, 18, 20, 22, 23, 24
Erwin and Peggy Bauer, 8
Joe McDonald, 10, 12, 14, 16, 20
PhotoDisc, Inc., 6

1 2 3 4 5 6 07 06 05 04 03 02

Table of Contents

head

legs

tail

Cheetahs

Cheetahs have a thin body and a small head. Their tail and legs are long. Cheetahs have yellow or tan fur with black spots. Adult male cheetahs can grow up to 7 feet (2.1 meters) long from head to tail. Female cheetahs are smaller than male cheetahs.

FUN FACTS

The black stripes that run from a cheetah's eyes to its mouth are called tear marks.

Cheetahs Are Mammals

Cheetahs and other mammals are warm-blooded. Female mammals give birth to live young. The young drink milk from their mothers. Cheetahs belong to the cat family. Lions and tigers also are cats. Cats can hear and see very well.

warm-blooded
having a body temperature that stays the same

A Cheetah's Habitat

Most cheetahs live in Africa. Only a few hundred cheetahs live in Asia. Cheetahs make their homes on savannas. They need open spaces where they can chase their prey. Africa is very warm. Cheetahs escape the heat by resting under trees or in tall grass.

savanna
a flat, grassy plain
with few or no trees

FUN FACTS

Cheetahs cannot pull in their claws. Claws keep a cheetah from slipping as it runs.

Cheetahs on the Run

Cheetahs are the fastest land animals. They can run 70 miles (113 kilometers) per hour. But a cheetah can run this fast only for short distances. It then must stop and rest. A cheetah's long legs take big steps. A cheetah's tail gives the cheetah balance.

balance
the ability to keep steady and not fall over

Cheetahs can go from 0 to 45 miles (0 to 72 kilometers) per hour in only two seconds.

Fast Food

Cheetahs are carnivores. They eat only meat. They eat small hoofed animals called antelope. They also hunt rabbits and some birds. A cheetah gets close to its prey. It then chases its prey and knocks the prey down. The cheetah then uses its strong jaws to choke the prey.

antelope
an animal that looks like a deer and runs very fast

Groups of adult male cheetahs are called coalitions (koh-uh-LISH-uhnz). The cheetahs in coalitions often are brothers.

Mating and Birth

Adult female cheetahs without cubs usually live alone. Adult male cheetahs often live with two or three other males. Male and female cheetahs come together only to mate. Female cheetahs give birth to young cheetahs about 14 weeks later.

mate
to join together to produce young

FUN FACTS

Cheetahs cannot roar. But a mother cheetah can call to her cubs with a chirping sound. The sound can be heard several miles (kilometers) away.

Cheetah Cubs

Young cheetahs are called cubs. Newborn cubs are very small. Their eyes are closed for the first week. Their fur is darker than their mother's fur. They drink their mother's milk for about six months. Cubs stay with their mothers for 14 to 18 months.

FUN FACTS

Some cheetahs have larger spots than other cheetahs. The spots run together to look like stripes. Cheetahs with these markings are called king cheetahs.

18

Predators

Lions and hyenas kill cheetah cubs. But adult cheetahs have no wild predators. People sometimes kill cheetahs. For many years, people killed thousands of cheetahs for their spotted skins. Selling or owning cheetah skins is now illegal.

hyena
a wild animal that looks somewhat like a dog

FUN FACTS

People can go on a safari
(suh-FAH-ree) to see cheetahs.
These trips let people watch wild
animals from short distances.
Most cheetahs do not hurt
people. They often come very
close to people on safaris.

Cheetahs and People

Cheetahs could become extinct. People are turning cheetahs' habitats into farms. But many people are working to save cheetahs. Scientists breed cheetahs in zoos. They hope to free these cheetahs into the wild.

breed
to keep animals
so that they will mate

Hands On: Cheetahs and Antelope

Cheetahs can run fast for about 20 seconds before they get tired. Try this game to see how quickly you become tired.

What You Need

At least three friends
An open space
A stopwatch or a watch with a second hand

What You Do

1. Choose one person to be the timekeeper. One person pretends to be the cheetah chasing its prey.
2. Everyone else pretends to be the antelope running from the cheetah.
3. The timekeeper starts the game and counts 20 seconds.
4. The cheetah must tag an antelope in 20 seconds.
5. Take turns being the cheetah, the antelope, and the timekeeper.

A cheetah can run 550 feet (168 meters) in just 20 seconds. It must catch its prey before it gets too tired. It will need to rest before it can hunt again.

Words to Know

carnivore (KAR-nuh-vohr)—an animal that eats only meat

extinct (ek-STINGKT)—no longer living anywhere in the world; cheetahs are in danger of becoming extinct.

habitat (HAB-uh-tat)—the place where an animal lives

jaw (JAW)—a part of the mouth used to grab, bite, and chew

mammal (MAM-uhl)—a warm-blooded animal that has a backbone and feeds milk to its young

mate (MATE)—to join together to produce young

predator (PRED-uh-tur)—an animal that hunts and eats other animals

prey (PRAY)—an animal that is hunted by another animal for food

Read More

Cole, Melissa S. *Cheetahs.* Wildcats of the World. Woodbridge, Conn.: Blackbirch Press, 2002.

Paige, Joy. *The Cheetah: World's Fastest Land Animal.* Record-Breaking Animals. New York: PowerKids Press, 2002.

St. Pierre, Stephanie. *Cheetahs.* In the Wild. Chicago: Heinemann Library, 2001.

Internet Sites

The Cheetah Spot
http://www.cheetahspot.com
The Wildcat Society—Cheetah
http://www.wildcatsociety.org/catalog/big%20cats/cheetah.html

Index